Through My Mystical Door

THROUGH MY MYSTICAL DOOR

A Collection of Poems Composed by

Irene Nutter

ARTHUR H. STOCKWELL LTD.
Torrs Park   Ilfracombe   Devon
Established 1898
www.ahstockwell.co.uk

British Library Cataloguing-in-Publication Data.
A catalogue record for this book is available
from the British Library.

ISBN 978-0-7223-3872-8
Printed in Great Britain by
Arthur H. Stockwell Ltd.
Torrs Park   Ilfracombe
Devon

I dedicate this book to my mum and dad, Betty and Jim, who sadly are no longer here, though I do feel that in spirit they have both lent a guiding hand in the writing of this book. Special thanks to my husband, David, for backing me; to my dear friend, Lorraine, and to my brother, Michael, for always being there; to Margaret for her friendship, and to Carole and Nubia for their kindness.

Contents

Through My Mystical Door

In my deepest dreams, o spirit guide,
Do take me with you to the other side,
To mystical realms through bounds unknown,
Through heaven's gates where seeds are sown.

To palaces of crystal bare,
Where loved ones meet with time to spare,
Carry me upon your celestial wings,
Show me an array of wondrous things.

Where domes of crystal and amethyst shine,
This other realm, just so divine,
Gardens ablaze with lavender and thyme
And the brightest red poppies all dancing in line.

Angels near, come hold my hand
And show me all your promised land,
Where celestial birds all flutter around
With song for mirth, all spirit bound.

Show me wonders, as yet unseen
In your land of wildest dream,
Where newborn babes with auras aglow,
And golden rivers of healing do flow.

Where sad souls are healed and new ones are born,
Start a new beginning from mothers' spawn.
Ready for a new day to dawn,
On God's earth plain to your mother warm.

I must return now, as my duty calls;
I'll awake in my bed when the telephone calls
Me back to this side, where I was born
In my mother's womb, so snug and so warm.

To remember dreams from so far away
On this so bright and distant day
Will keep my feet upon the ground;
'Til night returns, I'll sleep so sound.

My Mother

A truly beautiful being
She was in everyone's eyes –
A piece of gold
Put on this earth to bring a little sunshine
Into the lives of everyone's path she crossed.

A piece of gold never loses its radiance;
A piece of silver that has been gold-plated
Slowly begins to tarnish,
And eventually shows its true colour.

Gold people are God's special disciples.
Sadly we cannot change silver to gold or bad to good
Or the dark night to a sun-kissed day.

If you are blessed enough
To have a gold person in your life,
Then treasure that gift for all time,
For as long as your heart continues to beat.

To lose such golden treasures,
Sometimes bestowed on our beautiful world,
Must surely be sadness for all eternity.

A Dear Friend

You're as sweet as springtime
And fresher than air;
You're as warm and gentle as the summer sun.
You're always there.
Your aura is as golden as the autumn leaves
That flutter slowly down as angels from the sky.
I'll be your friend
Until the day I die.
You're as pure as the whitest snow.
You are God's gift, my friend,
And the nicest person
I could *ever* wish to know!

A Furry Friend

O Lacey, I loved you,
With white fur aglow,
Gentle fluttering eyes
Deeper than oceans can go.

So crystal and green
As the most perfect of jade
And as wide as the skies
That only God could have made.

I miss your muted bark
And your gentle whimpers too;
We were always together,
Just me and just you.

So wise and so loving
And forever there,
With your lead in my hand
Just take me there.

Do hurry now from behind that tree –
See, I told you so,
There's just you and just me.

Side by side we would snuggle
Beside the night fire's glow,
A velvet kiss on your forehead –
That was God's gift, you know.

My Guardian Angel

Sweet guardian angel, please be my guide,
And sometime take me to the other side,
Amongst God's lush and wondrous land.
O, stay by my side and hold my hand.

Carry me somewhere beyond the stars
That sparkle bright, somewhat like Mars.
To see my mum with hair so blonde,
With caring hands, with touch so fond.

To see the stars of quartz and jet
And precious rainbows of every colour yet.
From afar I glimpse a lustrous gate –
Perhaps it's amethyst and pure agate.

I dream of dreams so far away,
So pure, so treasured. Come close, this way –
Hold my hand and guide me there;
Take me with you, please be there.

Pendle Hill

Keep safe your memories, o, proud Pendle Hill,
Preserve them well, for it is God's will.
All things in life aren't for us to know –
Only guess, when seeds began to grow.

Adorned in summer with pink heather anew,
So rampant so wild and all covered with dew,
From morning to night you stand so erect,
With life's knowledge tucked into your world's parapet.

With prowess your paths freely roam your size –
Such beauty behold for one's weary eyes.
With witches galore and cauldrons alight,
Share so many secrets by day and by night.

On their broomsticks they fly with cats in tow
Out into the night where some dare not go,
Somewhere out there where angels don't tread,
Festooned with black hats upon their head.

Don't be afraid of the spells they cast
From witches' brews of herbs so vast.
They will not hurt you, or make you cry,
Just make you strong as hill so high.

Sleep now Pendle, for the day's been long,
Enjoy your dreams with joyous song,
For soon there'll be more feet that tread
Upon your tired and weary head.

The birds and bees the morn will bring
A host of wondrous songs to sing.
They'll scout for you from morning light
With dancing wings in star-filled night.

Wedded Bliss

Country bumpkin, I thee wed;
Soon I will take you to my bed.
To London Town or thereabout
For jellied eels, not tripe nor trout.

I'll have my say and you'll have yours,
Though not for ears beyond our doors.
We'll never quarrel, only cherish and care,
For wedded bliss will be ours to share.

Two babes you'll bear, both fair of face,
Blessed with God's gift, a saving grace.
One day they'll glimpse a guiding star
That shines so bright away so far.

You are so wise and as pure as snow,
A treasured gift I'll get to know.
You're an angel, my sweetheart I will love all my life;
I could never do better than have you for my wife.

From war days to hippy
We'll both flourish through;
With crimson flowers in your hair
I'll embrace my love on you.

Many years pass by with clock's ticking hand,
Let's waste no more time, dear.
We'll be as free as the cuckoo
To fly God's precious land.

Ingleborough

The early rising mist clings eerily
To the rich green slopes of Ingleborough.
A network of webs so gossamer-fine
Liken to a sponge of crystal spun sugar.

Awaken and rise, o, golden sun.
It's time to burn that morning dew
That spans the heathery velvet moor
And the countless miles of sweet meadows too.

The rush of the spiders
And insects alike –
For the rest of the day
They must hide out of sight.

A haven of petals
Reach out for a kiss of the sun,
As do the emerald leaves, all soft and lush,
For they too want some.

Your celestial splendour has spanned the years.
You stand so proud,
Beyond thick moors so soft and green.
You must have shed a myriad of tears.

The crimson sun sinks slowly down
As darkness brings its velvet cloud –
The mist o'er the valley
And village alike.

You too, Ingleborough, can sleep,
For I'll turn out the light.

Shadows of the Night

Why whisper my name in the shadows of night
When you could do it by day in the softest of light?
Come, hold my hand with touch so kind,
Show me a vision and I'll stay behind.

With loving help and tender care
Someday I know you'll take me there,
Where the sun burns the dawn and the darkness of night
And where treetop nests bed the birds from their flight.

Guide me through your astral realms
And soar above the skies so blue,
To eternity above soft downy clouds
On wings of doves and snowy owls too.

O, come with me, my love,
And take me with you far away
To a kingdom in heaven where my dreams of the night
Will stay precious memories for ever and a day.

God's Creation

The moon, the stars they shine so bright –
They're God's creation, a sheer delight.
They dance in time out there in space
Above white clouds with rich embrace.

Around in orbit they do go –
The days pass by so swiftly so –
With Saturn's rings of hues aglow
Aligned with Jupiter and Mars in tow.

To glance the moon when waning bright,
And wild abandon this dark night,
Guardian angels, with wings so fine,
Take me with you some place divine.

Queen of the Celts

Tara, Queen of the Celts you reign,
Adorned with robes and vibrant chain.
You ride so lithe over realm and plain;
Go find your King, he'll ease your pain.

Your horses tread the downy dew,
On moors across your precious lands;
Your followers – they seem so few –
Will carry you to God's safe hands.

Show me your castle built high on the hill,
Show me your clan and your strength of will,
For you'll overcome all wars and strife
And stay tucked away for the rest of your life.

Your roasting pigs on spits aglow,
And the crackle and pop from the embers below –
Enjoy your health and freedom so
For God bestows you land to sow.

Enchanted Woods

Enchanted woods with trees divine,
And becks all filled with deep rich wine;
Goblins chanting and fairies in flight,
There for all time, by day and by night.

Magpies and owls and woodpeckers too
All drink from the magical morning dew.
They sit atop toadstools round tree roots so deep,
Beneath leaves that drift down as jewels to keep.

A rainbow of colours so wide and so clear –
I must stay in these woods I treasure so dear.
A doe lies injured, so limp and so still –
Surely this cannot be God's will.

Hurry, fairies, and hover around,
Twinkling lights and spells profound.
Please save that deer you know so well,
And cast about a magic spell.

Sad eyes begin to open wide –
Saved again, my spirit guide.
Long velvet legs begin to move –
Put some weight upon your hooves.

Now gently into the forest go,
Find your mate, now don't let go.
No more sorrow on this bright day –
Go now, have your fun and play.

Thank you, fairies, for work well done;
Replenish your wings with God's bright sun.
Be ready now, when new day dawns;
Go spread yourself on ethereal lawns.

Babe

O, babe of mine, with cheeks so soft
And head aglow with golden hair,
Such nymph-like hands of gentle peach,
Angelic beauty, o, so fair.

All tucked away in womb so snug,
Awash with seas of food and love.
What a wondrous place it is to be,
Enveloped in womb of golden sea.

God's gentle fairies, wand in hand,
Translucent wings brush baby's hand.
Come forth now, babe, and see this world –
God's gift of love will soon unfurl.

Summer's Day

Red poppies that dance in meadows so bright,
Amongst buttercups and daisies, a sheer delight.
Hovering butterflies with gossamer wings,
Along with hummingbird and song it sings.

An array of wild flowers
And bumblebees in flight –
They gather their nectar
For combs they fill tight.

The sun's golden rays
Glimpse the waves on the lake;
Dance of ethereal colours, do so breathtake.
From sunrise to sunset, of red and of gold,
A rainbow of auras, a joy to behold.

God's Special Line

Mother, do you remember
I rang you on God's special line,
Where angels just lay there
With what seemed like infinite time.

Why in this world of sadness and strife
Do I have to spend the rest of my life?
Surely you could take me somewhere far, far away,
To a paradise in starlight with no night and no day.

With loved ones in heaven
All way up above,
The countless stars and the planets
Filled with your precious love.

No noisy response to my secret prayer,
Though deep in my heart I know you're still there.
A distant voice, the gentle touch,
A song in my ear means so very much.

Cinders

Cinderella to the ball,
I am the fairest of you all.
Coach by my side and glass slippers at hand,
Really it will be so grand.

O, hurry, please! I must be there.
I'm sure there will be time to spare.
Coachman, watch that bend –
Catch that wheel and it'll be the end.

That was close – a lucky escape –
With my trailing curls tangled up in my cape.
Still, don't be sad, we'll make it there;
The prince and I, we'll make a handsome pair.

Fairy Godmother, help me please:
Into these slippers I must squeeze.
Hurry now, quickly repair my curls –
I must get there before the other girls.

My prince, my prince, o, save me do,
For I know I really could love you.
O, Cinderella, my most treasured dream,
Trust me with your slipper, for you shall be my queen.

Enchanted Cottage

My chosen guides, fulfil my dream:
Enchanted cottage, fit for a queen.
With hares abound and doves galore
In that special place of old folklore.

Delphiniums and grapes upon the vine
Could this, God's gift, be really mine?
Mountain ash and spruce abound,
Make woodlands for fairies to fly around.

With spectral wings so gossamer-fine
Encircled with rainbows, just so divine;
Above the forests abundant trees
Awash with busy honeybees

Flutter down, crisp autumn leaves
And glance the rays of golden sun;
Caress the carpet underfoot
For magic spells today are done.

In twilight now my cottage keep –
I drift afar in land of sleep.

God's Own Land

The velvety darkness of night begins
And once again the curtain falls.
We drift away somewhere out there
On scented clouds and muted calls.

Come, fly with me to God's own land;
Stay close by me and hold my hand.
To charmed white palaces of crystal we'll go,
Just you and I and God will know.

We'll skim the fells where rivers flow,
Down through deep valleys with moorland aglow.
With buttercups, wild garlic, maybe hyssop and thyme,
We'll travel the world and be back by nine.

Time

The night is long,
The day is short
In this world – a mere port
In this universe,
Time is distant,
Time is now.
Today is the present
And tomorrow is yesterday.
A mere memory or a dream?
Do we really know.
There is autumn,
There is snow,
And priceless the little lambs
That soon grow.
The rivers run deep,
To the oceans they go
And then up to the sky.
It then comes to earth
To feed us until we die.

The Woods

Deep in the woods, so quiet, so hush,
A carpet of bluebells, all erect and so lush.
They dance around, as fairies would do,
Their bells with sweet scents of the morning dew.

A halo of primroses tucked deep out of sight –
The stream they guard by day and by night.
So proud they bathe in blades of green –
God's gift, a sight that must be seen.

Glistening raindrops sit as jewels on leaves
With veins so strong, but yet at ease.
Each will dance in breeze so light
As would the fairies in their flight.

Cygnets

Embraced with crimson from the west
Young cygnets wade and do their best.
They swim the lake of silk so blue
Embraced by reeds of deep-green hue.

Wiser swans stay by their side
And protect them from the open wide.
They span their pure white wings so proud,
As though embracing heavenly shroud.

Hovering fairies, blessed with eyes so bright,
Chant and sing from morn till night.
Wings they sparkle, as stars in the sky –
They'll be as guardians and stay close by.

The babes will grow and brace the snow;
With wiser eyes they'll get to know
To swim beyond the castle keep,
Or stay within its bounds so deep.

While eastern sun begins to rise
Above the soft rich velvet skies
Swans and babes will dance their tune,
Share happiness from morn till noon.

Your play must end, 'tis now dark night;
Stay tucked away and out of sight,
Surrounded now by mist and love
Watched over by a brace of dove.

Harvest Moon

Mountains laced with spice and gold,
As harvest moon be low to hold.
With autumn nigh on wing of prayer,
Let's climb way high upon God's stair.

Doves and owls, they watch close by
As angels dance through indigo sky.
With wings of silver glowing bright,
Up in the sky on this bright night.

Lustrous moon, for all to see,
God makes this world of harmony,
Where sphere of planets circle round
So vibrant, so clear – come, touch the ground.

A host of angels gather around,
Cup this moon and hold it sound,
Envelop their wings to keep it safe
'Til new moon comes, blessed with God's grace.

Crystal Ball

O, crystal ball, with eyes so clear,
Pray tell what future holds, my seer.
On spirit side you know so well –
Please don't make my life a living hell.

Speak to me, with tales to tell;
Show me your worlds, with tides that swell.
Make living worthwhile on this side too;
My friends help me live my life through.

Tomorrow will bring a glorious day –
Go live your life, be wild be gay.
Stay distant now, keep arms at bay,
For tomorrow will be another day.

Sweet Mother of Mine

Sweet mother of mine, I love you so;
O, why did you leave me and have to go
To the other side with loved ones dear?
I wipe my eye, which sheds your tear.

The days seem long, the nights worse so,
I reminisce such years of woe.
Though many happy times we shared,
O, thank you, God, my time's not spared.

Some day we will all gather there,
Hand in hand upon golden stair.
Angels will guide us to heaven's shore;
We'll spend all eternity after passing God's door.

Abigail

O, Abigail, with hair as silk,
With touch so pure you bear no guilt,
An angel from God, you're so divine,
This babe of fine spirit, o, child of mine.

God sent you to me, for ever and a day;
We'll spend many hours together and play,
With times of happiness and some sadness too –
For all time, Abbey, I will always love you.

You are God's special gift for me
From golden light, eternity.
We'll span the years that will unfold;
Cherish precious memories till I grow old.

One day you'll be my guiding star –
Maybe take me to other worlds afar,
To a better place than this in time.
I love you so, dear daughter mine.

Not For Ever

I cherish all memories of days gone by,
Though I'd lie in my bed at night and cry;
Such loving parents, though not here for long,
I lay deep in slumber, I dream of your song.

We see them as trees and the skies of blue:
For ever here, just for me and for you.
We never envisage that one day they'll go
To God's garden of love; we shall miss them so.

Lavender Dreams

Fields of lavender – some purple, some blue –
With essence of time and sweet scent of dew,
You scatter your seed for the world to see,
And create happy days for the wild bumblebee.

Reach out on your pillow this darkened night
And dance a dream in bright starlight.
Savour the sweet and magical spells;
Out in the night seek those mystical wells.

Dance now, float in dreams up above
To lands of honey, rich silk and much love.
Carry me there, stay so soft by my side –
You'll always be treasured, my dear spirit guide.

Father Dear

O, father dear, I love you so.
Remember those days of long ago
When you held me close, your breath in my ear.
You were so very special; I love you so dear.

So tall, so kind, my shining knight,
You kept me safe by day and night.
You forgot your worries and times of strife
By keeping me safe every day of my life.

A father as you I'll never forget,
Through twilight zones, where angels met.
To for ever stay beside me do –
Together in dreams I'm always with you.

Reach to the Realms

Full moon so bright as lasting sun,
Dark eyes behind soft swathes of cloud,
Deep in the night where day is done,
O, abandoned moon, you sit so proud.

Nestled amongst the Milky Way
With stars that burst with love so bright,
Your handsome glow to eternity stay
Sheltered by a host of angels this night.

Werewolf and witch, watch close to see
What spells are cast this night so bright;
On beaches so far out to sea
Go cast your spells in deep twilight.

Morning brings the eastern sun
With birds in flight that seek their food,
To feed their babes 'til day is done
And bathe in nests upon the wood.

Another cycle, now distant afar,
As wheels in motion spin so fast,
Reach to realms with guiding star,
Go rest with God; it's night at last.

Sands of Time

Sea's caressed by cascading light
On beaches of sand, such a shimmering sight –
Silken soft and fine through hand,
God's glorious gift, this chosen land.

To touch and caress the grains so fine
And shadows that stretch so far behind,
By sunlight at noon when sun is high
You can lie by my side till morning is nigh.

We'll roam the beaches hand in hand
And seek out life beneath soft sand;
Mussels and crabs and cockles a few
Will make food for love, and survival too.

Wedding Band

My husband, I love you, this far-distant day.
We've travelled world's heights and we're here to stay
Beside each other, warm, hand in hand.
I'll treasure for ever your wedding band.

It's gold and it's bright,
It shines this dark night;
Upon my finger it sits so fine
With veil and with headdress, so very divine.

This day of glory that now is done
Maybe you'll sire a beloved son
For all to see and love and hold,
We'll cherish for ever as a jewel or gold.

Rainbows

Celestial rainbows arched high in the sky –
A breathtaking blush I cannot deny
With purple and blue and pink and green,
The most glorious sight I have ever seen.

Such auras that dance in the dark stormy sky,
Above and beyond life's envious eye,
Surrounding our world for all to see –
A sight to behold, just for you and for me.

Rose Petals

Dual-toned rose petals, so velvet of touch,
Are sent from the Lord that we love so much.
He seems to know what's shared with love,
As celestial gardens, so high up above.

They're the richest pink shades
As strewn foxgloves on glades,
On thorny stems that reach so high,
On angels' wings to sun-drenched sky.

Lush green leaves that whisper on stems,
On winds of time that reach to glens –
One can never be sure, on this bright scented day.
Be happy, be joyous, and keep troubles at bay.

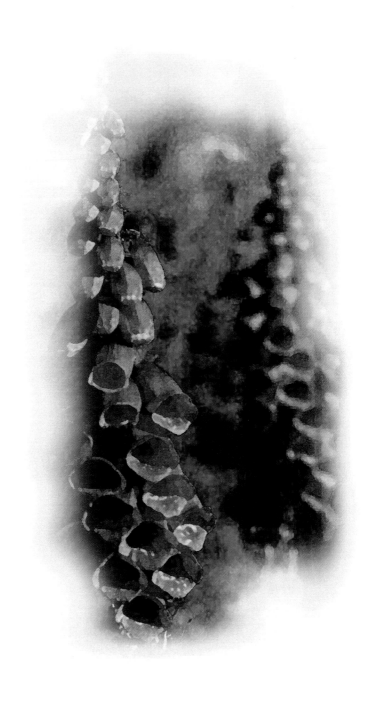

A Fairies' Abode

Treetops aglow with filtering light,
In swathes of silver, that dances so bright,
Highlighting contours of forests so deep,
Awaken now from your slumber so deep.

The toadstools, they swell as tables so round
That sweep the hush of the forest ground,
For fairies and elves on which to dine,
With seats made of ferns and sweet columbine.

They dance in the glades, and soak up the sun;
It feels today, that life's just begun.
A new day dawns and robins sing loud
As they dance with the fairies on bluebells so proud.

Over magical circles they hover so high,
They dance with agility up in the sky;
They'll cast their spells in wishing wells
And rest gossamer wings upon fragrant bells.

As night draws near, a doe deep in sleep,
An owl and a dove sit close by and peep,
To cast a watchful eye this night
To keep them safe, 'til morning brings light.

Limestone Hills

Limestone hills stretch far and wide –
You could take me there, my spirit guide –
Where rocks lay strewn as out in space,
Shed an ethereal beauty blessed with God's grace.

Outreaching valleys of fells and sheep,
Soft breezy downs with ferns asleep,
The rocks as white as passing clouds
And Celtic ghosts that tread soft grounds.

Gentle murmurs in my ear, from whispers on the silver birch,
With crows that caw, and hares that search
For food to feed young babes, alone
All deep in burrows beneath the stone.

Giant spruce protect the foss, with ethereal mist
For angels and fairies to bathe in bliss,
To dance on crags and fly the falls
Down to the pool and the cave that calls.

In gold and amber and the deepest of red,
The sun now departed has gone to bed,
As twilight now creeps down o'er the hill
To the shepherd's land, so quiet, so still.

Hill and Dale

I walked alone on paths of shale
Way up above the hill and dale,
On mountains, with tall peaks so bright
Under the moon and starlit night.

The call of the bird the morning brings;
With the essence of nature and song it sings.
They dart between the boughs so strong
To dance and play 'til the day has gone.

My tread so tender in peat so deep
That sinks like sponge beneath my feet,
All dusted with seed and twigs on the floor,
Make a carpet to enter a mystical door.

Angels in flight and lithe fairies too
All busy with much of God's work to do,
They carry lost souls from this side to theirs
To a place filled with love, in pure crystal lairs.

Good Spells

Cauldron, cauldron, steam and bubble;
O, why in this world is there so much trouble?
O, cleanse this world of sadness and strife,
And maketh for a happier life.

Hops and herbs maketh potent brew –
It is God's wish to cleanse a few.
To purity of life we're bound
To help all others this world round.

Come on, Alice, and do your work;
Make good for all and ease their hurt.
This spell abound could span all time,
But you must help and clear your mind.

Tomorrow will be another day
On this God's land so wild with play.
To realms we'll soar together true;
God's love could always be with you.

Don't Get Down

Don't get down on this wondrous new day,
For robins and skylarks all flutter and play
Amongst oak and ash, their song is so loud
Where the kiss of the sun burns the darkest night cloud.

With your head held high, be brave and strong
For tomorrow there'll be new chorus of song.
So high in the trees all scattered with dew
God's angels will always be here with you.

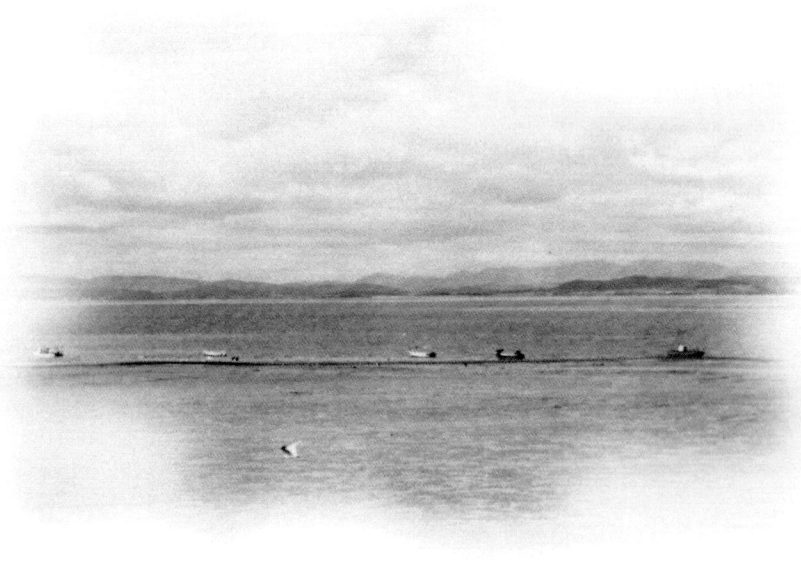

Golden Grains

Golden grains of sand so fine
Filter my fingers and span the time,
Encompassing beaches so broad and so fair,
Gives so much delight, just bathing there.

On seaweed, ripe crabs all scatter around
Amongst the cockles and eels wriggling round.
So lithely they move in their salty abode
Caressed by noon sun, about to explode.

Pounding the rocks and the dunes all around
The tide makes its mark with crescendo of sound.
A breathtaking sight, the scent does allure –
If I stay here this night, I'll be cleansed and so pure.

Woodland Down

Trees of hawthorn and hazel too,
Silver birch and leaves of yew,
All kissed with copper, green and gold,
Luscious leaves of youth unfold.

To sway in winds – some soft, some cold –
In woods on earth, with breath to hold,
Caress thy bark of trees so fine
That mark the years of measured time.

Somewhere hidden, lithe fairies dance
Amongst tall ferns they do enhance,
On a carpet of rich dark amber-brown
For hares to rest upon the mound.

Bobtail

Sweet bonny rabbit with eyes clear and bright
And bushy bobtail of brilliant white,
What did you do in the woods today –
Make a feast of wild oats and hay?

Crows in the sky all busy in flight,
Making their nests to sleep on this night,
With twigs in their beaks and lamb's wool too,
Will keep babes safe from fox and you.

Go lay your head on a toadstool or two,
Make sure that long ears are in comfort too,
Your babes in the midst of straw this dark night
All cuddled and safe to you mothers' delight.

Witches' Brew

Betwixt, bestow a spell this night
From cauldron round so deep and bright,
With flames aglow, so high, alight,
Tucked deep in the trees just out of sight.

This witches' brew it tastes so foul;
Stay close by me, wise tawny owl.
Watch and wait, encompass me
Whilst together we sit on old oak tree.

I'll cast my spell, o, wise old one –
Another day of work is done.
The fire's embers slowly die
As smoke disperses in night sky.

Seeds of Worth

With incandescent light so bright
Let's go soar the realms, seek planets this night,
On spectrums of colour with indigo too
'Tis God's way of showing how much He loves you.

Filtering the skies of such heavenly blue,
Hands reach out to me and to you,
Travelling time and spanning the earth,
'Tis time now, go sow your seeds of worth.

Shepherd's Day

Cascades of sheep adorn the fells
Of soft and luscious-scented downs.
Sycamore and birch surround the hills,
Tucked out of sight from distant towns.

By day they traverse heathery moor,
On heavenly land, through open door.
They drink the crystal water clear
From babbling brooks they love so dear.

Sun's rays cascade and glimpse the leaves
That dance on boughs of old oak trees.
The crows screech high upon their nest,
All stay the night for welcome rest.

Lone shepherd with crook in hand
Treads hill and vale the breadth of land.
So weary now from long hard day
Welcomes sleep on bales of hay.

The moon peeps bright just glimpsing cloud
And spreads God's light for angels high,
To spread their deeds and heal all life
And end another day of strife.

Another Day

The rising sun with watery hue
Peeps out from above the sky so blue.
Its glowing warmth as jewels and gold –
Prepare now, for another day unfolds.

Precious Rose

So precious you be, o, ivory rose –
Heaven scent, your fragrance glows;
Adorned with pert and waxen leaves,
Such pleasure gives and mind will ease.

Your blossom so fair –
An adornment for hair,
Enhance a special wedding cake
Or even a setting for an Irish wake.

Such lustrous rich petals
As velvet or snow,
A bouquet in God's garden –
'Tis his seed that doth grow.

Each bloom such size,
A blessed sight for one's eyes.
To caress you I must,
Treasure your sweet scent of musk.

You've been sent from above,
Made from God's special love.
An angelical sight,
Stay in my dreams this night.

By Your Side

So softly now I stand at your side,
Not in your world but the other side.
With your aura I blend
And God's love I send.

I am here when you're sad,
Sometimes, when you're glad.
Your aura bestow,
With pure love it will glow.

I'll be always in shade;
You need not be afraid,
Though my presence you'll feel
Just as though I am real.

In body I depart,
Though never in my heart;
We will always be together
To infinity, for ever.

Ethereal Rose

O, rose in slumber
Beneath deep-velvet sky,
Glanced by bright stars
And meteors that pass by,
Somewhere out there
In sweet heaven's abode
I treasure your gift
Of God's love to hold.

Old Mill Town

Burnley, Burnley, old mill town
With cobbled streets and chimneys round,
Clogs that clatter on alleys of looms,
Deft spinners and jennies all singing in tune.

Sweet lassies in pinnies and aprons alike,
Their hair curled up and out of sight,
From dawn to dusk they weave away,
So tired and weary by the end of the day.

They'd bathe by the fire in old tin bath,
Though cosy they were and all had a laugh.
With husband and babes and siblings too
They paraded in towels, two by two.

Morn brought the posser and mangle too –
There was always so much washing to do.
The Sunlight soap for face and clothes –
Must ne'er forget between those toes.

The Blink of an Eye

Gently I close my eyes
And drift slowly back in eons of time.
I remember events so long ago,
I even feel the trigger of the clocks' chime.

My heart seems to miss a beat
In recollection of times past –
Some happy, some sad.
There seem so many; it's just so vast.

Each blink is the shutter,
Each picture so real;
For some, I'm so sad I sigh.
O! God, can you really heal?

Now I open my eyes,
For I have scanned so many years.
Is life really a dream, just the blink of an eye?
So easy to remember those many deep fears!

I must cherish all memories, both good and bad,
And take life as it is and not be sad.
I blink my eye to wipe away its tears,
For life may yet hold many treasures in the future years.

Happy Times

Where are you, Father?
I miss you so dear.
Remember those nights
I'd shed many a tear.

I'd ride on your bike
With cushion on bar;
We'd go see the palace,
Though sometimes too far.

In big fancy cars,
With ice cream in hand,
You'd always show me
The Promised Land.

To the Elephant and Castle
And Leicester Square –
We'd share some eels
And have time to spare.

Back home we would go
With telly in tow –
A shock for Mum,
'Twas more work to be done.

I'd go to my bed,
Sometimes ache in my head;
Happy memories behold
In my dreams they'll be told.

Golden Thread

An ethereal thread that winds out there
And links us to a golden stair,
To crystal realms as yet unseen –
We travel there in wildest dream.

With angels and spirits
That traverse the limits,
To a port in the sky
Seen by only God's eye.

With my cord in tow I fly the night
And spread a little healing light;
To special friends and loved ones dear
In dreams I whisper in their ear.

Heal your sorrow in this starlit night;
With bygone spirits abound in flight,
This special place in time out there –
Someday I'll climb that golden stair.